D1321883

Facebook Business Basics: The Jargon-Free Guide to Simple Facebook Success

LEWIS LOVE

Although the author and publisher have made every effort to ensure that the information in this book was correct at press time, the author and publisher do not assume and hereby disclaim any liability to any party for any loss, damage, or disruption caused by errors or omissions, whether such errors or omissions result from negligence, accident, or any other cause.

Editing by Jade Matthews

ISBN: 1481214357
ISBN-13: 978-1481214353

For the people it helps.

CONTENTS

I'd like to thank those who I have worked with, without whom this book wouldn't be what it is. In particular; Louise for doing my networking for me, Jade for taking the time to point out my mistakes, and Adcocky, Maki-Moo, La Barbe and McDaddy for keeping me busy!

INTRODUCTION

The last few years has seen an explosion in the amount of content shared through social services such as Facebook, Twitter and Google+. Although search engines treat socially shared links differently than other types of links, they notice them nonetheless. There is much debate among search professionals as to how exactly search engines factor social link signals into their algorithm, but there is no denying the rising importance of social channels. The last three years has seen social media move from an uncertain strategy to an undeniable force behind the success of start-ups and established businesses alike. Every marketer now has their finger on the pulse of social media, keeping up-to-date with the latest offerings from Facebook, Twitter and Google+. No one has benefited more than small business owners and start-ups though. Social media plays a pivotal role in these businesses and this book will look at why that is.

It's important to point out at this early stage that marketing is not purely about boosting your sales. Sure, increase in revenues is always nice, but marketing encompasses many more parts of your business than you possibly realise. Marketing, especially on social platforms, affects your customer services, product development, merchandising and retail arms. You need to keep this in mind when reading this book and implementing advice, both techniques draw directly from here and from other resources.

My TED Talk

TED (Technology, Entertainment and Design) talks are a set of conferences that take place all over the world. Run by a non-profit organisation, Sapling-Foundation, the conferences aim to disseminate 'ideas worth spreading'. What this often leads to is emotionally charged speeches by some of the best speakers in the world, offering their ideas as the righteous path. This section will possibly sound like one of those TED talks. I make no apologies for this. Unfortunately, it has to be included, as too many people still believe in quick fixes and overnight success. Fuelled by the brainwashing power of moronic business coaches, offering '4 Steps to Quick Success' and 'Double your revenue with this one piece of advice', many entrepreneurs have succumbed to the idea that business is about growing quickly, becoming a millionaire and living off the fortunes you create. In reality, this seldom happens. Generally business is a slow, and sometimes painful process of growth and decline. The mark of a great entrepreneur or business owner is one that can foresee the decline, or at least prepare for it, and then recover effectively. Decline, I would argue is a good thing. It shows sustainability. Constant growth cannot continue forever; get used to it.

Business shouldn't be about the bottom-line. It should be about making the world a better place. If you can't look at yourself in the morning and say, 'my products, services or advice enrich or enhance the lives of others', I would question your motives. If you sell cars, are they roadworthy machines or just scraps of metal designed to get off the forecourt but not much further? If you offer advice on travel destinations, do you recommend places where you know the customer will love, or do you just opt for the easiest sell with the highest commission? Think about it for a minute, because if you were just going for those high-profit margins, without a care for the consumer, I would recommend you stop reading here. This book offers advice on how to enhance your social media, by giving, not receiving. Giving back to your consumers, providing free advice, sending birthday wishes without expecting to generate a sale as a result. It isn't about trying to directly drive your sales, although as you will see, this is a convenient by-product of your philanthropic, social efforts.

I've worked with some really talented people, leaders in their respective fields, and they all have a hunger to create the best possible products. These guys (and girls), needless to say, were all very successful at what they do. I've also been lucky enough to work with some people who are just passionate about the business they are in, not for making a profit, but for making their customers happy. A lot of people are like this. They care about their business, but aren't that interested in the product itself, especially when it comes to using it. Think of a stationary salesman; does he really have a passion for paper? You don't need to be that passionate about the products directly though; it's about being passionate about your audience and consumers. The paper salesman cares about his customers, so he sources the best quality paper for the fairest price, offering the greatest possible service. Paradoxically, he does care about his product, but that is only because he cares about his customers, who in turn, do care about the product.

A little while back, I had the opportunity of working with two great women, each of whom sold fine jewellery. For the purpose of anonymity, we'll call them Thelma and

Louise, although I would like to point out that neither of them have made a hobby of homicide. Well, not to my knowledge. Thelma imported her jewellery, selling them on her website and at specific events. Louise on the other hand, made all the jewellery herself. Obviously Louise's jewellery costs a tad more, but she also sold them through similar channels. They were both equally successful at what they did, targeting slightly different markets. What surprised me however, and opened my eyes to the world of 'doing good in business', was they both cared tremendously about their customers. I was expecting Louise to be somehow more 'in touch' with her customers and products, after all she made them (the product that is). I thought Thelma would only be interested in the profit margins - that is why you import isn't it? Well it turns out importing is a lot harder than it sounds. Thelma had to travel to India to source the stones, picking them each out individually. These then had to be drilled, cast or whatever other magic was performed before being imported into the UK. I was pleasantly surprised, and it made me realise, Thelma and Louise were both in the business of 'doing good'.

So how does this relate to social media and, in particular, Facebook? Well, we should care. We should care about our products and we should care about our customers. We should be 'doing good' in everything we do, and when it comes to social media, it's even more vital!

This book doesn't have the answer to getting a million, or even a thousand Facebook Likes. Instead, it's got some sound advice about harnessing the Likes you do have and making the most of your current fans. Think about this for a second; how much is a Facebook Like worth to you? Well if you've been working hard already, you may know how much traffic Facebook brings your site or business, the conversion rate of the traffic and a rough idea about how much each Like is worth. Great! If I give you a sneaky way to get a thousand more Likes though, do you honestly believe that conversion rate will continue? Of course it won't. As your engagement with the users drops, so does the conversion rate. What I'd much rather see businesses doing, is enhancing their conversion rates from their current social traffic; that way when new fans come along you're already set up to better help them, and as such, convert them. We shouldn't be preparing our Facebook pages and Twitter feeds for constant growth. Keep in mind that a bit of decline is probably just around the corner. This helps us to remember to look after the early-adopters, instead of just chasing after the new Likes. Social media, and business in general is a funny kettle of fish. I've waffled on about 'doing good in business', but then I also mention conversion rates and customers. It's easy to lose sight of it all. In reality, businesses need to make a profit, or at least self-sustain. With this in mind, conversion rates and customers are required; without them, we can't 'do good' at all. But if we remember, and make it our sole goal to 'do good', I'd suggest we could all make our own worlds a slightly more enjoyable place.

A Note on Social Media Managers

Whilst social media consultants can be worth their weight in gold, for small businesses and large corporations alike, I feel it can be a waste of money and ability to ask these experts to help with basic social media marketing setup, techniques and troubleshooting. That is why I have written this book; to serve as a handbook to those who feel they need a helping hand or a bit of advice starting out, and to also save them money that would have been spent on the experts.[1] This book looks at the basics of

---

[1] Note the use of the word 'Expert'. A good social media consultant can be worth every penny. They can help advance your position in the market through advanced social media

Facebook for businesses, offering itself as an introduction into a rapidly evolving field.[2] It is aimed at those who are bewildered by the social-sphere and need some friendly guidance in taking the first tentative steps into a world of Likes and viral campaigns. It may also benefit those who have dived into Facebook without assessing the situation first, serving as a rescue guide.

Social media managers can be a Godsend to businesses, especially for those that really have no idea what they're doing on social media. Social media managers should be experienced in all things social media, and they will be able to help you get on the right networks and create the best strategies to engage your audience and generate interest in your brand.

There are certain qualities that this individual needs to possess however. A social media manager needs to get into everyone's business. In order to know how to promote your company, they need to know what everyone in your office is working on and what their responsibilities are. An outgoing individual will have no problem reaching out to all of your employees and trying to learn more about what makes your office tick. Plus, outgoing people will be able to reach out and connect more with your social audience, which is the ultimate point.

Social media is not something that can be managed whenever - it needs to be managed constantly. Your social media manager needs to be hard working, so that they can spend their time: researching the best social platforms for

---

marketing techniques and I would be the first to endorse them. I'm slightly less enthusiastic about endorsing their services for setting up a basic Facebook page, something that, with the help of this book, you are more than capable of doing yourself.

[2] Facebook was only created in 2005. Prior editions, Facesmash and thefacebook.com were available before.

your business, creating accounts, creating an image for your brand on these accounts, and communicating with your audience. They need to answer questions and comments immediately, and they need to have regular posts in order to engage your audience.

Most of your social media postings are going to involve text, so it's very important that your social media manager knows how to write. If they can't string a sentence together, or if they misspell every other word, it's going to reflect poorly on your brand. Your social media manager also has to know what tone to use. Does your company want to come off as strictly informative, or do you want to be witty and humorous? It's very important that this is decided upon early on, and that your social media manager can convey the tone. If your company starts to mix up tones, it's going to be extremely confusing to your social following.

Social media is more than just Facebook, and it's very important that your social media manager knows this. A successful social media manager will have the knowledge and expertise needed to run a campaign on any network, and they can use this knowledge to help your business determine which platforms are the best options for your goals. Your social media manager also needs to know the line between public info and confidential info. Your business may have some information that should not be public knowledge, and it's very important that your social media manager does not share anything confidential with your fans and followers.

A social media manager can greatly improve the success of your company's social media campaigns. If you want to hire a great social media manager, make sure they possess the above qualities. I would suggest however, that this book should be able to bring you up to speed with all things social (especially Facebook), and of course as you immerse yourself with the social network, you'll pick up all sorts of knowledge along the way. This knowledge will be beneficial to you, whether or not you decide to outsource your social media management to a professional at a later date.

A Brief History of the Biggest Social Media Platform

Facebook arguably started when Mark Zuckerberg decided to create a college platform. Of course, he probably never thought it would become the overnight success it did. While attending college as an undergraduate at Harvard University, Zuckerberg experimented on a program which potholed campus students together for members to decide who was more attractive. The website was known as Facemash, which was later shutdown by the school administration for 'security issues'.

As a social networking site, Facebook has revolutionised the way in which people chat to friends and family, but it didn't start out like that. Notwithstanding the inconvenient incident surrounding Facemash, Zuckerberg began writing new code in January 2004 for a new website known as TheFacebook. Joined by his other colleagues in his own college dorm room, Zuckerberg wanted the site to help Harvard College students connect with each other. As computer programmers, Zuckerberg along with his four college colleagues; Eduardo Saverin, Andrew McCollum, Dustin Moskovitz, and Chris Hughes began using their skills to help students at Harvard create a closer tie. Their main aim was to create a web service that would help people share information by viewing profiles of people that are part of their network. The combined talent of these five men resulted in the creation of Facebook, which was first used by Harvard University as an online system for student monitoring and a steadfast management of online college-related tasks. TheFacebook, which was originally located at thefacebook.com, was launched on

February 4, 2004. In the first few days of its creation, TheFacebook was bombarded with controversies as to who the real founder was. Three Harvard students, Cameron Winklevoss, Tyler Winklevoss, and Divya Narendra accused Zuckerberg of stealing the idea from them, leading them to create another website known as HarvardConnect. However, the accusation did not prosper and the case was settled leaving TheFacebook alive and thriving. Its membership was initially limited to Harvard students but as its social advantage was realised, it was expanded to other colleges in the Boston Area, Ivy League, and Stanford University.

Opening peoples' mind to what is known as social networking, wherein people can build a personal profile and connect with friends across the planet, TheFacebook easily earned widespread attention from numerous audiences. A few months after it was launched, its expansion continued and it quickly became a growing phenomenon; gaining American colleges while gradually reaching most of the universities in Canada. TheFacebook expansion was so fast and trending that in a matter of months, it had gained 8 million users in the United States alone and was already expanding to seven other English-speaking countries. In 2005, TheFacebook dropped the word "The" from its name after moving its based operation in California and purchasing the domain name of facebook.com.

Back then, Facebook was limited to building personal profiles and viewing others' profiles, sharing stories through statuses and commenting on others, and connecting with friends. Its blue pages were made simple but its live chat features enticed more people to join, somehow outliving Friendster and MySpace. During the first few years of existence, the frictionless story sharing on Facebook led to numerous privacy and safety concerns among users. It was later discovered that kids as young as 13 years old were abusing its security settings. The use of obscene language and violent photos have also caught the company's attention, prompting them to build sturdier Facebook features and controls.

In March 2011, Facebook removed approximately 20,000 profiles from the site as part of a regular clean up for various infractions, spams, inappropriate content, and underage memberships. In response to the plight of members for a more secure and organised story sharing, Facebook finally rolled out its Timeline view in 2011. With a more refined privacy setting and enhanced user control options, Timeline made each user's Facebook experience even more fun and tenable.

From a simple college platform, Facebook has now become a worldwide phenomenon infecting billions of people with the positive (and negative) impacts of social networking. Since Facebook was launched in February 2004 however, it has changed enormously (along with its users). Facebook originally provided a variety of exciting features, which gradually added support to students in other universities. The basic yet exciting features included: being able to chat while online, receiving news feeds from friends within the network, connecting with friends, commenting and liking relevant statuses, and of course, creating pages. Along with other developments and add-ups, Facebook's popularity finally spread throughout the world, faring better than MySpace and Friendster, two alternative social networks that were also widely used at the time.

In December 2011, Facebook replaced Facebook Profile with Timeline, a new virtual space which provides users with more exciting features. With the new Timeline, users are able to upload and categorise photos, videos, and posts according to the period of time in which they are created.

In a 2012 survey, Facebook Pressroom recorded over 1 billion active users, 200 million of which come from the United States alone, while 50% of which are active users who log on to Facebook every day. From a simple school platform, it has become the largest social networking site, which currently plays an integral role in people's daily activities. Aside from being merely a social network, Facebook is now considered by many as an effective channel to market goods and services. Its global platform has given advertisers the perfect spot to spread the word about their products and influence thousands of buyers around the world. Politicians have also taken advantage of its wide coverage in winning over voters in presidential elections and organising protest movements. As a matter of fact, President Barack Obama used Facebook to get elected.[3] It has provided numerous opportunities for different companies to seek applicants, like Dell, who recruited new employees through Facebook profiles. It has also become the best venue for people to express opinions, vent, and share benevolent experiences by creating pages and cause-oriented communities.

Facebook has definitely made a great impact in the social status quo. Just as Facebook, Inc. wanted to preserve this, it continued to develop more features in Facebook, which do not only aid communications between people, but also allow them to enjoy and grow as an individual of the modern era. Although Facebook is blocked in some places like China, Vietnam, and Iran because of privacy issues, it now has 70 translations making it a popular website notwithstanding the regional and language barrier.

Facebook still has a lot more to offer in the near future and these are the things that many people are watching out for every day. At present, Facebook has over one billion users, more than half of whom are using Facebook on mobile devices. With the founder of Facebook, Zuckerberg, as the current chairman and chief executive of

---

[3] Well, it certainly helped him.

Facebook, Inc. the company's 2012 IPO and valuation of about $100 billion is considered to be among the largest in tech history.

Is Social Media Important?

No matter how hard you try to avoid engaging with the Internet, it is becoming a more and more impossible endeavour. It is through the worldwide web that people from different continents are becoming connected, how loved ones are staying up to date, how businesses are doing business. Almost all human transactions can be found online, be it relationships or purchasing, making the world more accessible and reachable than it was. So if you wish to have some power and influence amongst the crowd, you need to embrace the Internet and social media.

When it comes to business, it is very important to stand out and stay ahead of the competition. One sure-fire way to do this is by making an online presence and keeping it active. Businesses now need an online presence if they wish to really succeed, and starting out with the most powerful site on the Internet is a good place to start. Why? Because not only does it allow people to connect or network with each other, but now it also has special features for businesses to utilise, that they may market, promote, and advertise their services or products to the billions of users registered on the network.

Having a Facebook page has become an essential marketing tool for some businesses; it allows them to interact with their current and potential customers while also providing information and being entertaining. However, equally as many new businesses don't see the benefit of having a social presence. Some businesses feel that Facebook, Twitter or Google+ may not be right for them, but as potential customers lead an increasingly online life, the importance of having a presence on these sites grows too.

The thing to remember is, just because you have an account for every single social network out there, it doesn't mean that you will have more sales at the end of the month. It takes connection, an established relationship and consistency to be able to gain results. You also need to connect to the right kind of people, otherwise your efforts will drive awareness but not sales.

You also need to constantly inform your audience with timely and relevant news about your products and services. If you can, try to share information about other things that are not about you but still relate to your brand and products. You need to give them valuable information so that they can see you as someone of value.

Be wary of having to please too many friends and followers. They don't necessarily translate to buying customers. If you take a good look at it, what percentage of these people actually buys from you?

Even with this in mind, most marketers find that social media, and Facebook in particular, help them to create and market stand-out businesses in noisy marketplaces. Small business owners however, have many things to juggle in their time. One day they will be head of marketing, another day they'll be the chief financial officer, so trying to allow time for social media isn't always high on the priority list. Research has shown though, that building social media accounts is a great way to build long-lasting connections and brand loyalty. It probably won't turn your start-up into an overnight success, but it will help secure repeat business and steady growth for years to come.

The power of endurance is apparent when you talk to those who have been actively engaging in social media on a regular basis for three or more years. It's by no means a medium where you can see quick results, and for this reason, the social networking scene isn't for everyone. The important decision to make is whether or not you can invest the required amount of time, over an extended period. Too many marketers decide that Facebook is the way forward, give it a go, even doing it correctly, for six months, but then give up because they're not seeing the return on investment they were hoping for. Of course you do need to set a cut-off point - investing hours every week for five years with absolutely no return or sales to show for it isn't what you want, so set some targets and reassess as you hit or miss them.

FACEBOOK JARGON

From Posts to Friend Requests, social media sites like Facebook have created a language all their own that may sound like Greek to some. So before we go any further, the following list should clear up any confusion on Facebook terms. This list is by no means exhaustive, but provides a start for those who are unsure or new to Facebook and all its glorious terms. I don't mean for this list to be patronising, it merely acts as a resource for you to refer back to when reading the book if you are unsure on certain terms.

Add – As a personal Facebook user, you can add or 'friend' somebody on Facebook, acknowledging your connection to them. It's the personal equivalent of Liking a business page.

Cover Photo – This is the image that sits at the top of your profile. There are certain rules about what you can and cannot use this space for, such as price promotions, but you can get very creative with it. How about creating a timeline with key dates or using it to display a great picture of your team? You could even incorporate the profile picture in a clever fashion, so it looks as if it is part of the same image.

Events – This is an app on Facebook that allows users to let friends know about events that are coming up.

Fan – A fan is the equivalent of a friend to a business page. A fan can interact with a page, however the page itself cannot talk directly to the user on his or her wall. This is to stop spamming of users.

Friend –Facebook friends are often very different from your 'real-world' friends. Some people out of principle only become friends on Facebook if they are actually friends in real life, though this could lead to some awkward moments at work when your colleague realises that you don't actually like them beyond the working relationship! Friends on Facebook can interact with each other, view each others profiles and pictures and see each other's Wall posts, although recently this has become complicated by Facebook's privacy settings, as you can now set which friends see what.

Group – Similar in function to a forum or message board where the group members can share related content or media. Groups are a great way to connect like-minded individuals, such as networking groups or teams who would otherwise be disconnected.

Insights – This is where you can view your Facebook analytics data. You can get detailed information about your reach and engagement figures.

Like – Liking a Facebook page is similar to adding somebody as a friend. The user will see the page's updates and posts in their News Feed and will be able to interact with the page.

Messages – This is similar to your standard email, apart from it all takes place within Facebook. Messages are private and can only be seen between those who are writing it. Note that this can include more than just two people.

News Feed – The News Feed is what you see when you first login to Facebook showing you information including profile changes, upcoming events and other updates.

Notifications – Status updates, new photos, Likes, messages, how on earth do you keep up-to-date with all these goings on? Luckily, Facebook notifies you via the Notifications tab. When you're signed in and on Facebook, you may also see these displayed as a pop-up box.

Page – Brands, businesses, even celebrities should use pages, rather than personal accounts. Whilst there are some drawbacks, the benefits are far greater. By ignoring this, you risk having your business removed from Facebook. This entire book is based around your business running a Facebook page, rather than personal profile. If this isn't the case, I'd suggest swapping it (there is a guide on Facebook on how to do this).

Poke – Poking is a feature with no specific purpose. Because of this, and its stupid, and annoyingly juvenile name, I will henceforth never mention it.

Privacy – Facebook's privacy policy regularly comes under the microscope. You can put your privacy settings under your own microscope on the privacy page. It allows you to edit who can see what on your profile. I fully recommend that you at least take a look at this page, just to check that your settings are suitable for your needs.

Profile – Individuals have profiles, rather than pages.

Their public profile has since become their Timeline (previously known as Wall), along with everything else visible such as photos and 'About' sections.

Settings – All of that privacy stuff can be accessed in the settings, along with controlling other aspects of your profile.

Share – Facebook is all about sharing, but you can specifically share other people's posts on Facebook by using the share button. This then distributes that content to your friends too.

Status – A user's status is displayed on their Timeline and on their friend's News Feed. Users post messages for their friends to read. Friends can then respond with comments, as well as clicking the Like button.

Timeline – This is where a user's content is shown. Business pages also use the Timeline layout. It allows short messages to be posted, either by the user or business, or by somebody interacting with them. It is displayed in chronological order, with the ability to highlight certain posts.

Wall - The Wall was the space where a Facebook users content is shown. The Timeline has superseded it.

SETTING UP YOUR FACEBOOK ACCOUNT

It would be fair to say that if you are not yet making use of Facebook, the world's number one social media platform, you are a little behind the times. However, it is surprising how many people and businesses are not on Facebook. This may be because you are not a fan of the platform or of social networking in general, or it may be because you don't know how it all works. For these people, here is a beginner's guide to getting started on Facebook.

Before you can do much on Facebook, you will need your own account and user profile. The way to sign up is similar to the sign-up process for other social networking and online services. Follow these steps:

1. Head over to www.facebook.com
2. Sign up with your full name and email address, and come up with a user name and a secure password
3. You will receive a confirmation email. In this, there will be a link to click on which gives you full

access to Facebook
4. Done!

Setting up a Page

Setting up a business page on Facebook does not entail advanced technical expertise. Just by getting familiar with the new page design, you are already halfway there. Numerous small businesses have already thrived on Facebook. Taking advantage of the Facebook Timeline by setting up a business page is essential to getting your business started on Facebook. Listed below are the simple steps on how to set up a business page on Facebook.

1. Access the 'Create Page' button on the left corner of your Facebook page and choose the classification that best describes your business. The options include Local business or place; artist, band, or public figure; company, organisation, or institution; entertainment; brand or product, and cause or community. Classifying your business helps you rank in relevant Internet searches.

2. Complete your basic information by typing in your business name, brand name, or company name. You can also add your location, contact number, and other relevant information necessary to build an effective business page. In the profile photo, upload a high-quality image that best represents your business with an actual dimension of 180 x 180. Also upload a Cover photo that will best showcase your product services. Fill your 'About' page with a description of your company. Since this will serve as your main page, it is important that your company's description is succinct but creative, and reflective of the reason why audiences should visit your page. You may

also add your company's website to lead customers to your actual business page.

3. Manage your business page through your admin panel. It contains various features, which you may use to optimise and monitor your page. The 'Edit Page' button on the upper right corner of the page allows you to update your page info, change your company description, or upload another profile photo or cover photo. You can also use the admin panel to change the role of your administrators; for instance if you have assigned some employees to respond to comments and other relevant queries.

4. You then need to build your audience by filling in your page with exciting information about your products. Feature in your page your product pictures, product updates, client testimonies, or link to your product reviews. You can also use your business page to alert your potential customers with the latest special offers, events, and discounts. Inviting more fans and contacts to like your page should come after there has been good interaction on your page. The more strategic you are in managing your business page, the larger audience you will gain.

5. Monitor your Facebook on a daily basis. Leaving it unattended after setting up a page is not enough, as we will see throughout this book. Considering the pace of time, your business page should continue to thrive and compete with other businesses. To check on how fans interact on your page, you can check on the page's own analytics. On the upper right of the 'Admin Panel' you can reply to private messages sent to your page. On the upper left, you can also read the comments from your audience and respond to them. Ignoring these people isn't advised as it will

adversely impact your page.

After setting up a page, your next priority should be familiarising the features of Timeline to sustain an exceptional marketing strategy and strengthen lead generation efforts. Depending on the business niche you have, you may create multiple Facebook business pages and drive a lot of traffic from over one billion Facebook users. However, creating multiple pages requires a lot of time and effort and shouldn't be a decision that is made lightly.

The Difference between Pages, Groups and People

Gone are the days of being able to easily explain Facebook's features. In years gone by, when you signed up to the site there was only one type of account, the personal account. Specially designed for individual use, its main purpose was to connect the user with their friends or people they know who have also created profiles at the same time. This allowed every user to get updates of the latest happenings or events of each other's lives without having to contact them every now and then; either through snail mail, email or expensive phone calls. But as business-minded individuals discovered the potentials of Facebook for networking and marketing, it began to evolve into a bigger version of itself. Currently, aside from people's profiles, the network also provides Facebook pages and Facebook groups. So what are these Facebook pages, groups, and people about? How do we distinguish one from the other?

Starting with the most basic, Facebook people (also known as a Facebook profile) as previously mentioned is for individual use only. So if you are a real person and want to connect with friends on Facebook then you can create a profile. A Facebook profile allows you to stay connected and interact with other people very easily. You can get the latest scoops on your friends, send them private messages, tag them to events or pictures and post statuses of what you are currently thinking so that they may also know about it. It's worth noting that these types of profiles are reserved purely for individuals, not for businesses. Facebook does allow you to convert your personal profile into a page though, so if you are currently using your personal profile for business use, I would recommend converting it pronto! Facebook have been known to delete profiles that are being used for business use.

Facebook pages, on the other hand, are for public figures (bands, celebrities, and public officials), businesses, organisations, and other entities who want to create a public presence and provide information or updates to fans in an official, public manner. They are purposely made to be visible. Therefore one can connect with them anytime by Liking the page or becoming a fan, and instantaneously the latest news about them will be fed on the subscriber's Wall. The only requirement for making a page is that it should be created by an official representative of the public figure, business, organisation, or entity. Similar to profiles, it also needs real people and names, because once Facebook finds out that the page is not legit, they will remove it immediately without notice.

Lastly, a Facebook group is for people who share a common interest; be it a cause, an issue, an event, or any topic there is. It is like a forum or message board where the group members can share related content or media. Since it is halfway between being a private profile and a public fan page, administrators have full control on the group's privacy setting. They can either make it public but require approval for persons to become members or keep the group private and invite only those people who they think should be part of the cluster. I use this type of page regularly for creating networking groups and for business ventures with groups of people who might not be connected in other ways. It helps to create a team atmosphere amongst people who would otherwise feel disconnected.

Making Your Facebook Page Look Great

Facebook Timeline gives business individuals everything they need in one easy-to-manage system. With the new virtual space, it becomes easier for users to: monitor their brands and social feedbacks, engage in better customer relations by publishing content across multiple profiles, filter the most relevant information from the hundreds of conversations through the News Feeds, and measure the company's overall effort through Facebook Insights or Google Analytics. Despite all of this, so many companies have shoddy-looking pages.

According to the latest survey, Facebook has become the top most-visited website, with over one billion active users all over the world. Thus, a great Facebook page is crucial to attracting millions of potential buyers every day. Considering the number of potential buyers that can view your page, you definitely need to beat the hundreds of competitors with a great Facebook page. To make your page look great, listed below are some points that you should be focused on.

Adding your company's name sounds obvious, but many Facebook pages don't even seem to have a clear name. You should obviously be using a unique name for your business or company, possibly one that will outline the nature of your products or services. Since your brand name will appear on the top part of your Facebook landing page, it is best if your name is catchy and creative, based on your own original ideas. Of course, you may already have a brand name, in which case I wouldn't recommend changing it for Facebook (more on staying consistent later). Along with your brand name, you'll need to add some information to the 'About' section. There is a limit of 165 characters, so avoid long-winded tales of how you've fought off demons and risen above evil emperors to bring your customers a fairly plain product. Instead, be succinct and to the point. That being said, comedy can really work here, so you may want to include a small reference to demons and evil emperors!

The first impression on any web page is almost always visual, so uploading a high-quality photo that is relevant to your products or services can really help. It can be an image of your products or models with your products, depending on the type of business you are running. By all means, you may edit your profile image before uploading it to enhance its overall impact and be able to bring a uniqueness that will attract viewers. While Facebook requires profile images to be at least 180 pixels, it would be best if you format your pictures to the correct aspect ratio before uploading to avoid a distorted or pixelated image. Along with your profile image, which is seen most by users, Facebook also now allows you to upload a Cover photo. This image sits at the very top of your Facebook page and can create a real visual impact for anyone visiting your page. You may want to consider hiring a professional photographer and designer to create this, although if you're savvy with photo editing you may be able to do this yourself.

Whilst we're on the subject of Timeline, it's worth noting that you can backdate posts. This is great for long-established businesses that are new to the world of social media. Rather than looking like the new kid on the block, fill out your timeline with old images, important dates in your company's history and other such information that can give you the respect and distinction you deserve.

Adding Facebook applications to your page can enhance your page's functionality and can bring quality to the content for your viewers. Using the static FBML (Facebook Markup Language), you can add a welcome tab for your viewers. Through the list of Facebook applications, you can also add widgets that will link your viewers to your blogs or other relevant websites, such as Twitter, Tumblr, YouTube, and many more. Using the static FBML is a little bit further than this book will be going, but if you're keen to learn about it, or find somebody who could do it for you, there are a few links at the end which will point you in the right direction.

Google analytics is a tracking system that will help you know the number of people who visit your page and the places that they came from. While 'Facebook Insights' gives a demographic view of Facebook interaction between your fans, Google analytics provides more comprehensive statistics. Using Google Analytics is also the easiest way to track your sources of traffic and top keyword searches.

To attract more viewers and make fans stick to your page, you should not only maintain a great Facebook page but also a good flow of communication with your fans. We'll cover important information about driving traffic to your Facebook page a bit later, but it's important to remember to interact with your fans on a daily basis by attending to their needs, answering their concerns, and solving their problems. Do not limit yourself to solely selling products, but engage in a long-term relationship with your clients and extend your influence by inviting friends. Lastly, provide a place for your clients to give feedback and suggestions, which you may use to enhance your page and customer appeal.

USING FACEBOOK IN YOUR ONLINE BUSINESS STRATEGY

As the economy gets tougher, business is becoming more and more competitive and cutthroat. To make a name for your brand in such a hostile environment takes careful planning and an effective marketing strategy to make sure you are heard and appreciated. The same planning and strategy will help drive your business forward in terms of sales too. With that being said, for small businesses, multiple advertising and marketing streams are just not possible, so when given the option to choose just a single advertising method to promote your business, what should it be? Well, with over a billion members worldwide to date and laying claim to the spot of top social media platform there is, Facebook has to be considered.

In a recent survey that looked at how small business owners were using social media marketing in their online business strategy, there was a surprising trend towards using traditional marketing strategy techniques alongside their social strategy. Many businesses planned to use email marketing and event marketing with most using press releases to get their message across, as well as using outposts such as Facebook. I think this is an important point to remember; whilst Facebook is on everybody's mind, it's easy to forget more traditional methods of promotion. It's therefore important to keep these going alongside any social strategy you are planning on implementing. Facebook isn't the 'answer' to every business's marketing woes; it merely acts as another place to project your message. Using Facebook along with other promotional techniques will help your business to grow, but to do this you need to make sure you have a good strategy and plan in place. This part of the book looks at how you should develop your Facebook strategy to maximise the impact of your campaign.

Creating a Strategy for your Facebook Campaign

Just joining Facebook and talking to your fans isn't enough. You need a strategy if you want to succeed. Just like we create business plans, sales forecasts and growth targets, Facebook needs a thought-process to work. Creating a campaign needn't be hard though; it's just about setting down your goals and how you plan to achieve them with the help of Facebook. For some, social media is about creating a buzz about products or services. Others use it to keep in contact with their existing customers and add value to their service. By keeping your goal in mind, you can create your campaign fairly easily.

Make sure your campaign offers value to others. A nice trick to creating a great social media campaign is to think of how you can help others, not yourself. The common sayings about social media; 'sharing is caring' and, 'be sociable, like us', are testament to this. Social media is about being social, not about being a salesman, so make sure you are sharing content that is valuable to others. Try to provide information that solves problems that your fans have and offer incentives for people to connect with you.

Of course, you could provide the best incentives to Like your company page, but if the content you share isn't of good quality, you'll have people disconnecting from you just as quickly! It's really important that the stuff you're sharing is of the highest quality and to make sure that as much of it as possible is original. If you only share tech news that is produced by the BBC or CNN, why would people Like you instead of the BBC or CNN? Original, quality content can really define your business as a leader in its field. Creating innovative content is a great way to get people to notice your business. Dull and boring content will be skimmed over, but by having a unique voice, with ground-breaking content, you'll be putting yourself ahead of the competition quicker than you would think.

Remember to give yourself a breather from time to time to keep your creative juices flowing. You might not realise it but a simple Tweet or Facebook shout-out can already be taking too much of your time. It can also stress you out. Just thinking about a clever Tweet or an attention-grabbing status can take a toll on you, especially if you expect yourself to do this several times a day. Worst-case scenario is you burn out and you stop posting altogether. Sometimes, you get a light bulb moment, but you are not in the position to publish it, so you wait until later and then you lose interest. You might end up with random, scattered posts that are useless and irrelevant to your audience. If you find yourself in this position, it would be wise to schedule your posts so that you can have a level of consistency in your social networks. We'll cover a bit more on consistency, and the importance of it towards the end of the book.

Finally, once you've got your head round what you're going to be doing and how you'll be doing it, you need to devise a plan to measure your results. As I've previously mentioned, you can't always expect huge gains overnight with social media, but you do need to track your progress. There are hundreds of tools to keep track of your social media campaigns, from Google Analytics segments to tools designed specifically for social media management and tracking, such as HootSuite. Ultimately, it's about finding the tool that provides the right amount of data for your needs, in an easily readable format, which won't take you hours to compile each month.

A successful social media campaign can often be defined as how carefully you are listening to your users. Feedback given by users is essential to building your campaign, and as such, growing your business. Pay attention to your audience, as they know what they like better than you do.

Driving Traffic to your Facebook Page

Before a company can use Facebook as an extension of their marketing, they have to generate traffic to their page, and this can pose a challenge to businesses that are unsure how to do this. In order to generate traffic, you need to promote your Facebook page. This section details some of the ways to increase the traffic, in order to use Facebook to its full potential.

Your website is a hub of information for your business, and most of your customers will have visited your website in order to learn more about your company. Using a Facebook widget, you can easily inform and link your customers to your Facebook page from your website. You can choose different widgets—there's even one that has a Like box so your customers can Like your Facebook page directly from your website.

If your company sends out email blasts or newsletters, make sure that you let your subscribers know that you now have a Facebook page. Again, you can use widgets that allow you to send these individuals directly to your page, which will generate traffic. Another good idea is to make sure that you add content before your widget, to tease your subscribers about what they can find on your Facebook page. Knowing what your page has to offer will entice them to click through.

Chances are you send a great deal of emails on a weekly basis, and like most businesses, you probably have your contact info placed in your email signature block so your customers can easily get hold of you. Think of your Facebook page as an additional contact method, and add a link to your Facebook page in your email signature. This puts a link to your page in front of anyone who reads your email, whether or not they are already a customer.

Many companies are using contests through Facebook in order to generate traffic to their page. This is a great way to get your company name out there and build a fan base. Your contest can be something lengthy that contains a phenomenal grand prize, or it can be something smaller that occurs on a weekly basis. You can hold a photo contest, ask trivia questions, have your customers make suggestions on products—anything can be turned into a contest, and as long as it is run smoothly and follows the Facebook guidelines, you will easily see a jump in your Facebook traffic.

You can use a portion of your marketing budget to invest in Facebook advertising, in which an ad for your company's page will be placed on Facebook, allowing current and potential customers to learn that you have a page and Like it. Facebook ads allow you to reach your target audience within your own budget, and it's a great way to generate traffic to your page. There's more on Facebook advertising in the next section.

Once you've made a great Facebook page, use these tips to boost traffic to your site and generate a large fan base. Just make sure that once you have these fans, you continue to generate engaging content in order to keep them.

Using Events to Promote Your… Event

Facebook Events is an app on Facebook that allows users to let friends know about events that are coming up. Friends use them to publicise birthday parties and gatherings, naïve teenagers use them to announce their house party details to the world and professionals use them to discover networking events in the local area. These events can be Public or Private, something that teenagers organising house parties rarely know, and can detail location, start time and even a guest list of who's going, something that teenagers organising house parties always know. Private events are found by invite-only, whereas those that are public can be seen by anybody. So public events are often used by businesses to promote their own events. From shop openings to grand sale days, events are a great way to spread the message about any interesting events you've got planned. They are a great way of connecting with your fans and target audiences, inviting them to events and getting the event into the social-sphere.

Of course, just like everything on Facebook, you can't just dive in and create an event, expecting thousands of people to attend. You need to plan your strategy carefully, drafting out how you intend to promote the event and your timeline for doing so. Sending out invites should be the first thing on your to-do list after you've created the event. By inviting all your friends, you can jump start your campaign by asking those closest to you to attend. Of course, don't go spamming your personal friends with business requests. If your best friend doesn't like fashion, don't invite him to your fashion show that you are planning to launch your new clothing store at. Instead, pick those friends who are actively interested in what you do. By picking those who are more likely to attend, your event will have a stronger 'Attending/Maybe/Not

Attending' (AMN) ratio. This information is displayed to all invited guests and because, as humans, we all like to follow the crowd, a high number of 'Not Attending' guests may signify that the event is not the sort of place most people would be seen at. Getting a great AMN ratio early on will actually make your event more attractive to invitees.

Once you've invited your friends and you've given them a couple of days to respond, it's time to spread the word to the rest of the world. Start on Facebook by 'Sharing' your event with the fans on your page. Again, give them a couple of days to respond before moving onto the next platform. Now is a good time to start to incorporate other methods of promotion. Stepping out of Facebook will allow you to attract fans that are not currently connected with you. If you've got an email list, create a mailshot with a tool such as Mailchimp. Setting up a mailing list is easy and involves minimal cost – you can then use it to promote your events. This goes for other outreach tools such as blogging and Twitter.

You don't need to exert blood, sweat and tears to promote your event however. You can utilise social adverts directly on Facebook too. Every time somebody RSVP's on your event, their name will also appear alongside your advert, making it a lot more enticing for their friends. Facebook advertising is covered in a bit more detail further on in this book, but it's worth knowing that this is an option. It's also worth knowing that I have ordered this section of the book into the order in which you should promote your event. That is, invite your personal friends first, then your Facebook fans, then step out of Facebook; targeting those who already interact with you and your brand, finally targeting people who don't know about you or your brand through Facebook advertising. The reason for this is simple: growing an event slowly will make it easier for you to keep on top of questions asked within the event and keep your AMN ratio looking great!

When your event gets a bit closer, you may want to send out a reminder about the event. People lead busy lives, and although many seem to be constantly connected to Facebook, some of us only check it once a week. Your fans might forget what they RSVP'd to or simply when it was. A friendly reminder will drive the rate of attendees up no-end, but be careful not to spam your fans. You might have an event on every weekend, but I'd recommend thinking carefully about inviting every fan, every week to these events. You'll very quickly lose your fans if they aren't interested. This brings me to remind you about the restrictions of geographical location. Yes, where a fan lives is going to have a big impact on whether or not they attend your event. Online, you may have fans and customers from all over the world, but are they really going to be able to attend your event in the rolling British countryside?

Converting Facebook Users

With the largest number of users around the world, Facebook poses a great opportunity for many business owners to gain a lot of customers. By using a good marketing strategy, it is easy for you to convert active audience into highly engaged website visitors.

Converting Facebook users to loyal customers does not only entail posting ads, creating tons of posts, and uploading hundreds of pictures. After hitting the Like button, it is not uncommon for most fans to not come back at all unless they have good reason to. In converting Facebook users, your first goal should be to give potential customers a reason why they should love your business page.

Hard selling may suggest a lack of creativity and induce boredom in potential buyers. Upon seeing the same phrases, such as 'Work from home, earn extra money! Click here' or 'You are the last winner for today, click here,' customers would no longer want to visit something that is not unique, or is just churning out the same content as other sites. To convert Facebook users to regular customers, you should be focused on three things: adding value to your network, boosting credibility, and building trust through a competitive campaign. It is important to make a point - you are not just selling your products, but you are also willing to give back to your customers by providing them with valuable information, maintaining good relations, and sustaining good page interaction.

Don't just collect Facebook fans like trading cards. To convert them into avid buyers, you need to give them reasons why they should become one. Make them feel that they are a part of your network by giving incentives, such as free coupons, free samples, or free eBooks. Make your business page even more engaging and enticing by celebrating milestones, hosting games, sending 'thank you' e-mails to regular visitors, and trying out sponsor stories whenever applicable. You can also highlight positive testimonies and feature compelling photos from fans to show that you place customer happiness above gaining a profit. The more you give back, the more Facebook visitors will come back and stick to you.

Unlike hard selling, tagging on a call-to-action gives room for creativity. Connect with your visitors and convert them to loyal customers through a combination of call-to-action and offer variations, including enticing content, appealing design and style, and easy accessibility. Make your call-to-action scheme concise, engaging, and clear. Letting your fans know what is available for them right on your business landing page will motivate them to explore your page and check on your products.

Find the right tool to measure your Facebook stats; most preferably the one that can integrate online and offline shopping channel information, measure your weekly or monthly progress, and assess your competitor's progress as well. You can also experiment on data mining and data analysis to have a comprehensive report in measuring your progress. Updating your records on a daily basis will help you know the number of people visiting your page, the number of fans converted to customers, and the number of purchases which are crucial to rate your conversion progress.

When converting Facebook users to customers, it is important to maintain close brand monitoring and sustain a good marketing strategy to uphold the desired results. In order to know which method works best for your brand, try these tactics and measure your business page's effectiveness. Take your Facebook marketing strategy to a whole new level one step at a time.

FACEBOOK ADVERTISING

Being the world's largest social networking platform doesn't come cheap. Over the years the creative geniuses behind Facebook continued to innovate and create interactive features on the network which allowed people to make their thoughts and ideas known to the world. Financing such a huge network has always been challenging. Social networks that require payment from the user rarely work well, but littering sites with adverts are just as much of a turnoff. The team at Facebook have worked hard to allow advertising to boost their revenue, but at the same time minimise distraction to users. Of course, if every user ignored every ad, nobody would advertise on Facebook. Therefore, the social giant has been quietly placing adverts in clever places and targeting them to the right audiences, so paid advertisements blend effortlessly into the rest of the content from friends and family.

Facebook advertising started in August 2006 when they signed a three-year contract with Microsoft. The agreement allowed the Microsoft Corporation to place international ads on the social network in exchange for revenue split. This move turned out to be successful - by the last quarter of the year 2009, Facebook announced that cash flow had finally turned positive for the first time. This meant that consumers could continue to use the site for free, with the ads bringing in billions of dollars annually – enough to sustain the Facebook team who continue to maintain the social network.

Facebook advertising has really helped small and local businesses recently, allowing them to target specific groups of people or those who live in a certain area. Anyone can start their own business nowadays and not worry about how and where to start selling their products or services. As a foundation, they can sign up for a Facebook account, amass some friends or followers, and *voila*, business is good to go. This section of the book looks a bit closer at the types of Facebook advertising, allowing you to work out which, (if any) would be great for your business.

But before we go any further, what can Facebook advertising do for businesses? Will it actually benefit your sales and commerce? Well, like the advertisements consumers were exposed to back in 2006, Facebook ads have changed little. They are however arguably better than more traditional forms of advertisements and online 'banner' ads, both for consumers and businesses. The first reason for this is because they occupy slightly larger screen real-estate than other types of web advertisement, thus giving more exposure and details to its readers and increasing the chance of turning them into leads. Second is that aside from the information, businesses are allowed to include their logos or images on the ads, making it attention-grabbing, if not recognisable. Lastly, before they are broadcasted, the company who owns the advertisement gets to specify the characteristics of their targeted audience. Using this, Facebook gathers information from their database, finding the users who fit the given criteria, and then showing it to them on different occasions. Because the advertisements are in their area of interests, the possibility of them clicking on the ad is high.

Sounds good, but how much will a business need to spend to run an advertisement campaign on Facebook? Well, there is actually no definite value when it comes to this, because the amount you pay solely depends on how much you are willing to spend. First you will have to determine if you want to pay per click (CPC) or pay per 1000 impressions (CPM). Then the network will ask for further details about your campaign, before providing you with an estimate of the cost. With CPC, the average fee is only £0.20 per click. But depending on the bids, how huge your advertisement and campaign is, and its click-through rate (CTR), you will either pay more or less than the approximate calculation. Once the deal has been made, the advertisements will then be made visible to identified users at the right upper side of their Facebook accounts.

Lastly, Facebook advertisements are classified into two distinct formats: the first is the standard Facebook ad and the second is the Facebook sponsored stories. Both kinds can be featured on the user's Facebook profile for a fee, but they do differ slightly. That's what we'll look at in the next section.

What's the Difference Between an Ad and a Sponsored Story?

Facebook ads are not much different to the other ads you see posted (all) over the Internet. These adverts are what give the social network's users free access to use Facebook. So, how do Facebook ads work?

It's simple. A business designs their ad and uploads it to Facebook. They point out what specific groups of people they want their ad to be shown to by using demographic targeting and then pay Facebook for its publication and distribution. Consequently, the social network identifies and pairs the ad to users they think conforms to the client's given criteria and only flashes it to them on the right side of their Wall. Now it's up to the user to check out the ad, or if they don't like it, they always have the option to close or dismiss it by clicking on the 'close' icon provided at the very top of the ad banner. But how about sponsored stories? Many tend to confuse them with Facebook ads. What are their differences?

Sponsored stories are comparable to the News Feeds you see from your friends because you only see them when people you know have interacted with certain pages, applications, events, and even ads. Thus, it is similar to getting updates from friend activities; only it involves some sort of business advertising. A more accurate description for sponsored stories would probably be 'highlighted'. Whether you would be interested in the promotion or not, because your friends have interacted with them, the advert will be highlighted on your Facebook account.

To summarise, both Facebook ads and sponsored stories are delivered to consumers for a fee to the advertising company. This is how Facebook pays their bills and allows its users to use the social networking site for free. Therefore, enterprises can share content with a larger audience by taking advantage of Facebook's billion users. Facebook ads are shown to people who fit the descriptions of the business's targeted audiences. So when setting up an advert, you can target the audience so that your ad will catch the interests of users. On the contrary, sponsored stories can be ads, pages, applications, and events that your friends have interacted with. They're a great tool to enhance your position on Facebook by targeting like-minded people to those who already love your brand.

What are Facebook Offers?

Facebook offers are one of the latest and arguably most effective advertising platforms you can take advantage of when you have a Facebook business page. By creating

Facebook offers, it is easy for you to bring people to your business. These offers can be in the form of coupons, discounts, contests, or promotions, which you will post on your Facebook page or send via email to your selected clients. Once your client clicks on the offer, it will direct them to the exact location of the offer.

There are three basic offers available to use; in-store only, online only and a combination. 'In-store only' offers are suitable for business owners with retail stores or physical business locations who do not have online stores. Some businesses may have a Facebook page, but do not necessarily sell their products online, such as groceries and supermarkets. Using this offer, you will have the chance to promote your retail or grocery store online. When a buyer needs to redeem the offer, he or she may present a printed coupon or an email to the staff at your business.

'Online only' offers are well suited for businesses that do not have physical locations and are solely intended to market online. This works well for online stores selling fashion accessories, apparels, and footwear, although it's not just a service restricted to those examples. Using this kind of offer will give buyers the chance to redeem offers online and transact business via the Internet by using coupon codes or barcodes.

Out of the three, the 'combination' option is the most flexible kind of offer. This makes it ideal for businesses with an online store and a physical shop. This can also work for hotels and resorts or travel businesses, for instance in giving room discounts or travel promos. Thus, when a client who isn't close to your physical location redeems a discount for hotel accommodation, he or she can simply claim it online or show it once they arrive at the location. This also gives clients from other places the opportunity to take advantage of your offer, regardless of distance.

The choice of offer can vary wildly depending on the

type of your business and your budget. Facebook offers an 'estimated reach', which will allow you to choose the number of people who will see your offer in their News Feed. On setting the budget, you may use the suggested budget on Facebook or customise your own budget. The more people you want to reach, the more money you may need to pay.

When making an offer, the most important things to consider are budget, suitability, and appeal. Before making an offer, consider the total profit of your business. If your profit is too small to make a big offer, do not place your business at high risk just for the purpose of availing Facebook offers. It is also important that you design your offer in a way that suits the type of business that you have. Choose the one which you think is most effective and compatible for your business. Lastly, design an offer that is appealing for the audience. Although your offer may have reached millions of Facebook users, no one would care about a lousy offer.

A good offer should be beneficial for you and your buyers. Consider the great numbers of competitors - your offer should contain the things that your clients want the most, in order to grab their attention.

Facebook offers are only available for Facebook pages with at least 400 Likes. If you have less, you can earn more Likes by inviting friends, or read the section on *'Driving Traffic to Your Facebook Page'* again, to gain more Likes before setting up a Facebook Offer.

THINGS TO REMEMBER

This book has covered a lot of the basics, and as much as I love to think of it as the Holy Grail for those who are new to Facebook, I also must admit that from time to time, things don't always go to plan. This section of the book looks at some common mistakes people make when starting out on their maiden Facebook voyage, and how best to avoid them. The majority of these mistakes are just due to inexperience and therefore can be easily rectified. It's for this reason that I believe the following chapter to be the most important in the book. Some of the information is quite obvious when you think about it, but I have been asked countless times why fans aren't connecting with a page that only posts content about products. Perhaps it's not so obvious. Either way, read the following chapter carefully and take it all in. I promise it will save you money in marketing consultancy fees and improve your social accounts overall. The majority of this section goes for other social platforms too, not just Facebook. Whilst there are differences between how you should post on Twitter as opposed to Facebook, many of the underlying principles remain. Being aware, sociable and consistent are all things to remember on any social networking platform.

Be Sociable

People join Facebook to be social, not to be sold at. The number one mistake small businesses (and big businesses) make on Facebook is 'broadcasting' your messages to fans, rather than interacting with them and providing them with relevant content on a continual basis. The main job on Facebook for your business is to interact and be sociable, not to sell. If your company isn't being authentic, or is just trying to sell directly to a fan, people will see straight through it and move onto someone else's page.

It's sometimes difficult to explain this in a way that is easily understandable, so I sometimes ask people to think of it in a 'real-world' way. Imagine you are chatting to your friends over a few drinks after work. You're sat in a trendy bar in the centre of the city and there is some music playing in the background. You're enjoying catching up with your friends from your school days, when one of the bar staff pops over and asks if you want to buy more drinks. You decline, saying that you're ok at the moment, but may want some more shortly. The bar staff leaves without any further conversation. Then, exactly one minute later, the same member of staff approaches you asking if you want some food. You explain you've already eaten and you don't want anything else. Again, they leave without saying anything else. They come back two minutes later wanting to know if you want another drink. Hang on - you told them only three minutes ago that you didn't want a drink, why would you want one now? Even writing this is starting to get me annoyed, so we'll stop here by unanimously drawing the conclusion that you wouldn't stay for another drink. In this analogy, the company's Facebook page is the bar and you are the Facebook page's fan. Just like you'd leave the bar, and probably wouldn't return, you'd probably 'unlike' the page, and have no intention of 're-liking' at a later date.

You can see why it's important not to over-sell to your fans. But surely by not pushing the hard-sell, you won't see any gains? Well if we continue to use the bar analogy, how would you feel if, in the same situation, the bar staff were polite, courteous, even sociable? I've been in bars where the bar staff are happy to advise on drink or food choice, listen to my ramblings, join in conversations and even exchange jokes. Needless to say, these bars keep my custom. Now if you applied these principles to your Facebook page, you'd be taking big leaps in the right direction to create a great Facebook experience for your fans. Provide relevant and handy information - just like the best bar staff will tell me what wines go with what food. Chat to people about their social life, especially if it is related to your products or service industry. You could even go as far as to tell jokes. A joke a week might be gimmicky, but if you could relate it to your industry or products, even poking fun at yourself, you can really build your trustworthiness and authenticity on Facebook.

Many companies want to use Facebook to make more money, but by engaging with customers and providing an authentic, meaningful online experience, people will begin to feel a part of a community and be more inclined to spend with you at a later date. Facebook isn't somewhere to drive quick growth within businesses, but it can help you to organically grow your brand to an audience that cares and matters.

Be Consistent

Have you got a logo? Have you got a colour scheme? Have you got a tagline? Have you got product images? Have you got promotional images? If you're missing any of these, stop reading now... You're still here? Ok, now are they all consistent? Does your logo match or compliment your colour scheme? Does the tagline work well with promotional images? Are your product photos clearly part of your brand?

Your online presence needs to be consistent, especially your imagery. Due to the nature of small businesses and the way they evolve, owners often find themselves with two or more logos that they use, or taglines and promotional imagery that were created after the logo. Try to keep everything consistent, especially across platforms. If you're on Twitter and Facebook, make sure people can easily identify you on both. Don't use one set of colours for one, this is not how to A/B test![4] So the focus here is why businesses should stay consistent with their content and branding on Facebook.

There are three specific things that should remain unchanged when marketing your business on Facebook: first is the logo, next the brand colours, and lastly but perhaps most importantly is the relevant content. Logos have been used for years by companies and institutions to symbolise their brand, their message and to represent what they do. This is because it is easier to remember an image, through the power of association, than a name. People may effortlessly dismiss a long and unheard of company name, but with a logo they are more apt to identify and recall it. Just think of the famous golden arches, an image which is of course related to McDonalds, or the distinctive tick mark of Nike. Whether their exact names were printed under them or not, once you get a glimpse of the logo you know what businesses they resemble and what they are

---

[4] A/B testing (sometimes known as split testing) compares the effectiveness of two versions of a particular product to work out which one is better. This can be done by looking at conversion rates.

good at doing. So keeping your logo consistent is vital to building your brand. Many people use the social-sphere to build brands; therefore a logo that remains constant should surely be at the top of your priority list.

Moving on to the brand colours; you can readily choose any colour you like to be incorporated into the logo and brand guidelines, but with careful consideration and reference. Colour can have a huge impact on how effective your business's logo is. Studies have shown that colours have different effects on people. For instance, the colour red is associated with increased appetite. This is the reason why most food chains (think about McDonalds again) have shades of red not only on their brand's image, but also inside their restaurants. If you wanted to represent your company as environment-friendly or as fun and carefree, then you could opt for green or blue.

Lastly, but most importantly, is the relevant content. Since we are talking about Facebook and social media marketing, relevant content is essential. The more your audience gets from your business, the more they're likely to give back. It will not only give an inside view into your business, but it will also help you to achieve a good rank on search engines and gain you popularity amongst followers who are ultimately going to keep your business alive. Once put together, the logo and brand colours contribute towards the marketing strategy of your business, and by combining this with excellent, relevant, timely content, you can ensure that people will remember your brand for years to come.

Be Aware

Social media is one of the hottest topics in human resources management at the moment – and given the human fascination with information, gossip, and all the latest news, it's no wonder that social media sites have launched into the stratosphere of the Internet over the past few years. They're where our friends and family are – and they're also where our News Feed resides, as well as being the place to catch up with what our favourite celebrities are saying. In fact, if you sat down the average person in front of their preferred social media site, chances are they could easily spend an hour or more there without getting bored. In short, social media has become a big part of our lives. But how does our fascination with all things social media play out in the workplace? Well, for many, it simply doesn't – a recent survey suggests that over two thirds of UK business IT administrators have banned staff from accessing Facebook via their work computer. Being aware of these statistics is important for anybody who wants to engage with their fans. If they are all caught up with work, it's probably not a great idea to try and engage them in deep conversation. The reasons companies ban workers from using Facebook could of course be to do with reasons that are purely practical – some network administrators may not want people streaming video and using up precious bandwidth. The other thing to note here is that the web has gone mobile – so limiting or blocking access from a desktop computer doesn't necessarily mean that the organisation has banned its staff from checking their social media feeds.

Given the statistic above, it may seem at first glance as if business leaders disapprove of social media – but the picture is a bit more nuanced than that. In fact, a recent survey suggests that nearly half of executives believe social media has a positive impact on workplace culture. So it seems that within some organisations there remains a question about whether social networking adversely affects productivity, whereas in others there is no block on its use. Of course, the important thing with social media in the office is striking the right balance. By developing a policy, employers can help ensure social networking is used appropriately. This means, for instance, that employees have a clear set of guidelines regarding what can be said about the organisation.

As the mobile web increases its reach – which it is doing with each new model of smartphone that's released – social networking policies will need to be refined and in some cases even rewritten. Interestingly, one study even suggests that people would take free use of social media in the workplace over a higher level of pay. One thing is for sure – social media has changed not just the web landscape but also the way we express ourselves as people.

Remembering this is important for anybody setting up a Facebook business account. How freely can users interact with you? Are there times when your fans are more likely to engage with your content? The last thing you want to do is be (part of) the reason for getting one of your fans fired!

Troubleshooting Your Facebook Plan

Whether you're using social media for business or for your own personal gain—or even if you're using it for both—it's possible that you may become overwhelmed while trying to stay up to date with all the new networks that are out there. If you're experiencing any of the following frustrations, it might be that social media is overpowering you.

You have too many accounts.

If you have signed up for every social media account out there just to have a social media presence, you are going to be overwhelmed. There is no reason to be on every single social network, and it certainly won't automatically lead to more sales at the end of the month. It will take too long for you to gain a following, and you won't find the time to connect with your following on each one. It takes connection, an established relationship and consistency to be able to gain results. You also need to connect to the right kind of people otherwise your efforts might drive awareness, but you won't see any increase in sales or engagement.

You also need to constantly inform your audience with timely and relevant news about your products and services. If you can, try to share information about other things that are not about you, but still relate to your brand and products. You need to give them valuable information so that they can see you as someone of value. I know that value is something that has been repeated throughout this book, but I can't stress how important it is to running a successful social media campaign.

It's also important to be wary of having too many friends and followers. They don't necessarily translate to buying customers. If you take a good look at it, what percentage of these people actually buys from you? This should also be noted if you were thinking about buying Likes. Don't do it.

You don't have a social media plan.

If you're using social media for business, it's an extension of your marketing efforts. For this reason, you need to have a plan in place. This plan will help you determine how you want to use social media, who will be in charge of your accounts, and what your overall goal is for using it. If you don't have a plan, you will not have any structure to your use, and you won't know what you want to gain from using it. If this is you, flick back to the section on *'Creating a Strategy for Facebook Marketing'* and read it again. Everything you need to know to get started is there, use it!

Your only social media postings are automated.

Automation tools like Hootsuite and Sprout Social allow you to schedule posts and updates for your social media accounts. If you are only on these tools to schedule your posts and are never on the actual social network, you're never having real-time conversations with your following. This can have a major impact on your overall social media success. Social media is meant to be social, not completely automated.

You don't post.

Automating is one thing, but being completely obsolete on social networks is another sign that you're stuck. This means that you either don't take it seriously, that you don't know how to access the accounts or that you don't know how to use them once you're on them. There are some resources at the end of this book that will help you through the basics if this is case.

In terms of time, Facebook marketing for small businesses doesn't have to be that consuming. You can have an incredible social presence for as little as six hours per week investment. That's less than one day a week. Of course, in the early days of your foray into the social media world you won't need to spend quite as much time on Facebook. It does take time to build an audience, both your own time, and time in general, but stick with it and you will start to see some real results.

You post too much.

If social media scares you, you might feel the need to share every detail about your life or your business through these channels. If your followers know what your employees arc wcaring, where they ate for lunch, and what time you clocked out, you're sharing too much. Over-posting is a sign that you don't know when to stop, and this is a major sign that you need to take a break.

Don't post for the sake of posting. If you have nothing good to share, just don't post. Avoid trivial posts such as stating where you are at the moment, unless it's an important event that your customers must know. Don't post if you are just going to say that you are in the supermarket or you are looking for a cheap toothbrush. Don't schedule content that sounds like you are trying hard to be present online when you are really not. Instead, make sure you have a nice balance between scheduled posts and spontaneous posts.

You have nightmares about social media.

Social media should not take over your life. Instead, you should use it to gain a following and, in turn, follow those who are important to your personal and business life. Use social media to generate awareness about your business and connect with your customers on a more personal level. If you would rather sleep next to a Puma than talk about social media, it's a sign you need a break.

It's all you think about.

If you spend hours trying to come up with the best tweet or post, you're trying too hard. Creating tweets and posts should not be a time-consuming effort. You need to use it to share relative information that your following will find interesting. If you write and rewrite posts, you're putting too much thought into it, and you need to take a break.

Social media is meant to give you a way to connect with friends and family and allow your business to connect with customers and industry experts. If you find yourself falling into any of these categories, it's a sign that you're completely overwhelmed by social media, and you may need to take a step back in order to reassess your efforts.

Your Business Doesn't Fit into Facebook

While you may be fluent in your own language of architecture or plumbing, you may be struggling to work out how Facebook would fit into your online marketing strategy. Plumbers are one such group of people who often struggle to fashion a Facebook plan for themselves, often regarding Facebook and social media as completely foreign to them. But it is a language that can help you hear conversations about customer needs and even create a way to reach new customers.

For professionals who are used to talking with their tools, getting started or reaching out to a potential client they don't know can be challenging. But once you get the conversation started, it is hard to stop. Thinking outside the box is key in such industries, but to get you started, here are a few ways to dig into the world of social media and heat up the conversation for such sectors.

Joining groups is a great way to connect to like-minded individuals, including customers as well as your competition. These groups are bundles of like-minded social media users, all posting to the same pages, sharing the best practices and offering tips. By subscribing to group updates, you can be a part of a conversation that could bring you more business, or help you offer services more smoothly to a larger population.

Social media not only allows you to tap into the whole world in one place, but it also allows you to grow your home turf, starting conversations on a local level that you may never be able to have in person. The Internet breaks down many social barriers, for example, allowing plumbing contractors to discuss issues with neighbours, and there is no reason why other local businesses cannot use Facebook in this way too. Chat with other local business owners; befriend networkers who may know someone in need of your services, and work to make introductions online that you can turn into in-person meetings.

Once you have created a social media presence and have gotten the hang of posting, it is time to start the conversation. While your social media friends and connections may not be your average customer, reacting to their questions, commenting on posts and starting conversations of your own makes you seem like an online authority in your field. By engaging in conversations online, you can make yourself the local expert in your industry, and that can translate into sales, as friends begin to trust you as an authority on the subject. Don't be afraid to express your opinion. It could really pay off for you in the long run.

WHAT NEXT?

So you've (almost) reached the end of the book. You've successfully followed it through and are now looking at a great-looking Facebook page, with a fair few fans that are growing every week. You've cracked the biggest social network and you want to know what to do next. This section of the book tells you exactly that. So without further ado...

Staying on Top of Facebook

There is more to Facebook than simply creating a profile. Facebook allows small businesses to thrive by bringing in leads, opening greater possibilities, and increasing sales. With Facebook marketing being one of the most effective and cost efficient ways to reach out to billions of potential customers, it can be a place where your success story never ends.

Registering to Facebook and creating a profile is not enough to convey to your audience that your product is good. To stay on top of Facebook marketing, you will have to create a good marketing strategy. To start with, you need to learn about time discipline and management. As a business professional, time is a precious asset, so you need to engage with your customers in the most effective way. Create a time management system that will help you carry out the business operations of your Facebook page. Begin by planning out your entire week. You should be able to list all the important things that you need to accomplish within the week. Although other people may consider to-do lists old fashioned, it remains to be a great way to keep track of your weekly tasks.

Next, integrate your to-do list in a time planner or schedule. Here, you can lay out the dates when you will visit your Facebook page, update your status, upload videos and photos, cater to comments, messages, and suggestions, and respond to notifications. It is crucial not to spend too much time updating your Facebook page. Despite your busy schedule, you should be able to give time to your customers and make them feel valued. Thus, your schedule planner will help you keep track of your tasks.

As part of a good marketing strategy that will keep you on top of Facebook marketing, you should know how to use the Facebook features. With the new features of the Facebook Timeline, you can implement a better system for posting to Facebook. After you have created a post, you can broadcast your content just a little louder to guarantee that you are seen and heard by your target audience. Listed below are the top Facebook Timeline features that you can implement.

- Pin a post – Pinning a post allows you to manually choose a specific status to stay up on the top of your Facebook Timeline for at least seven days. You can choose this feature to broadcast offers, promos, and other significant announcements that you want your audience to easily spot.

- Highlight a post – Highlighting a post expands your status update across the Timeline page. Since it guarantees wider viewing, it poses a great advantage in drawing more attention to the most important content of your page. As a good highlighting strategy, you could highlight good customer testimonials and other posts that promote your products.
- Promote – This new feature from Facebook allows your post to be seen by more of your audience than usual. Once you click on the 'promote' button below your status bar, your post will be prominently shown on top of your friend's News Feeds. The only downside of this feature is that you will have to spend a fee for it, but it does generally guarantee wider audience coverage.

Climbing to the top of your Facebook marketing potential will take time, as it also entails effort, discipline, and creativity - especially when it comes to time management. Nevertheless, once you have conquered your Facebook marketing, you will realise that all your time and effort will eventually pay off. All you have to do is maintain time management and a creative Facebook marketing strategy to maintain your position.

Building a Blog

A blog is one of the most effective assets of many business professionals. Almost every business establishment already has its own blog to increase visibility and keep in touch with billions of potential customers. A blog can also be considered as a successful leeway to show your passion and exhibit relevant information, essential for business growth.

Building a self-hosted blog with your own domain

name offers more of an advantage for your business than you might have imagined. Customers prefer doing business with the experts. By working hard on a blog, you can showcase specific skills that will transform you into a recognised expert within the market. Through your blog, you could also show a more comprehensive review or details about your products for your potential customers. You can also use it to tell the story of your business, share your personality, and position your business in a unique manner. As a blog targets specific human elements, it is easy for you to show which field you are specialising in and attract your target audience.

Blogging is the easiest way to update and connect with your customers. You can use it as a channel to upload content that will help your customers know about the latest products available, the progress of the company, and the current promotional offers. Refreshing the contents of your blog on a daily or weekly basis is also an art of publishing that will build trust in each customer. Once you gain trust, customers will keep coming back to your blog, follow instructions and ideas, and will buy the products that you recommend.

Using your blog, you can position your business in a unique manner at a lesser cost. As part of a good branding strategy, you can use your blog to build an identity that shines among the rest with a good logo, a slogan that conveys the purpose of your blog, unique but simple designs, excellent product reviews and updates, and other valuable information. Blending creativity with a good marketing strategy will make your blog crucial to viral marketing. Once you are able to build a unique branding strategy, your blog will become your tool to spread the word about your business and gain more customers. It is worth noting that a blog works efficiently as a way of interacting socially with the rest of the web, which will help you to tap into the global mind and reach a wider coverage of customers in just a matter of minutes. It will not only amplify your purpose but could entice billions of customers to try out your business.

Blogging is not just pure business; it can really be fun too. Your blog can be an exceptional tool to give your clients some incentives, such as promotional offers and coupons, and entertain them in a creative manner. You can make use of your blog to initiate games, contests, or raffle draws to market your product in a more engaging way. A blog that can awaken positive emotions, such as excitement, happiness, and contentment will provide greater benefits in gaining new customers and making old customers stick with your brand. When you engage with your customers, you will gain their loyalty, which in my opinion is the most crucial achievement of any business professional, much more so than simply making money.

Blogging itself is self-fulfilling. Once you realise your full business potential, more and more creative ideas will eventually appear in your mind. In effect, your blog can be the best tool to sharpen your intuition, focus on the wide variety of unique branding strategies, and uphold the loyalty of your customers.

Learning LinkedIn

LinkedIn is one of the fastest growing social networking sites, whose focus is on connecting people with their business associates, clients, and former colleagues at work. Launched in 2003, LinkedIn has been uniquely known to network people professionally.

But who says it is only limited to professional networking? With greater functionality brought by its new features, LinkedIn is currently being used by numerous entrepreneurs to expand their online business and market their products. Creating a LinkedIn profile is a wise move to allow your business to business (B2B) marketing to reach a new level of effectiveness upon entering the new era of data-driven marketing.

Since LinkedIn offers a business-oriented and update-based platform, B2B marketing can highly benefit from its faster company promotion and more enhanced visibility. LinkedIn can be an exceptional marketing strategy to allow potential customers to research your company and see if they are interested in doing business with you. In return, you may also conduct research on other companies to discover competition, potential partners, and new suppliers to better know your position in business. Through LinkedIn, you may assess your strengths and weaknesses as you compare your standing with other business establishments and create a special marketing strategy to climb on top of B2B Marketing.

LinkedIn also offers a variety of features that can increase the overall appeal of your business. The redesigned 'Company Page' allows you to share updates and reach your target audience, which are essential elements to build a better business that may lead into a deeper relationship between you and your clients. With its streamlined design, you and your client can search through a more organised category of information, such as company news, career opportunities, products and services, brands, career goals, and insights. Through the 'Company Follow Widget', you can also drive people into your company profile and make new, valuable connections. More marketing features such as the 'LinkedIn Signal' and 'Skills Endorsement' tabs increase the coverage of your company by allowing you to monitor LinkedIn feeds, communicate with first-degree connections, and allow others to endorse you based on your specific expertise. Once endorsed by other users, you will have higher chances of selling your products, gaining more customers, and establishing consumer trust. Like Facebook, its new 'Banner' photo allows you to display your company logo or company cover to establish identity on LinkedIn, which adds to the branding possibilities.

The LinkedIn Company Page, which can now be accessed through iPhones and Smartphones too, poses a great advantage to mobile users. Business professionals coming from America, Europe, India, and China who are reliant on mobile technology can access LinkedIn and respond to client needs wherever they are. This feature paved the way to a more speedy response system, making potential buyers stick to specific businesses online.

At present, LinkedIn records more than 152 influencers, many of whom are prominent figures such as Barack Obama and LinkedIn's owner, CEO Jeff Wiener. With these people on your connections, your story can be more than just an update. Applications like videos can also tell your company story and create a multimedia experience with other users. When told in the right way, your story can also serve as an inspiration and create a deeper connection with your clients.

LinkedIn is considered to be the home of business professionals, where people do business at a professional level. When it comes to introductions and updates, users observe stringent LinkedIn etiquette to maintain professionalism. With less personal gossip and extra-careful users when it comes to product reviews and comments, B2B marketers can rest easy, safe in the knowledge that LinkedIn offers a safe and secured environment.

Pinning your hopes on Pinterest

The latest trend of business today is obviously towards the online realm. Haven't you been reading the book? In moving from the traditional buy-and-sell technique to the most impressive online marketing strategies, small business have taken advantage of social networking to gather more visitors and boost sales.

Recently, Pinterest has been gaining a lot of attention

from small and large businesses alike. Pinterest is the third fastest-growing social networking site next to Facebook and Twitter. Its visually oriented platform gives a unique appeal to products and is helpful for targeting specific clients. With over 14.9 million unique visitors, Pinterest can be a good asset to enhance your online business.

There are many ways in which Pinterest can help enhance your online business. Although it may not be quite as popular as Facebook and Twitter, Pinterest's visual approach has captured a specific type of person, which you cannot find on other social networking sites.

It can be the best venue to run contests and engage with customers in a personal and cost-effective way. After creating a business account on the site, you can 'Pin' photos of your product offers, coupons, freebies, and other exciting offers like trips and raffle draws. Since the site has higher work vitality, your pinned images have higher chances of getting repined, and therefore reaching a wider audience. Surveys show that 10% of shoppers who surf through Pinterest are more likely to buy products that have authentic and fascinating product photos pinned on a Pinterest business page.

Aside from merely maintaining a blog site, you can also use Pinterest to spread the name of your product by pinning interesting pictures. You do not have to write lengthy articles, create call-to-action statements, or experiment on catchy phrases, which are already very common today. With Pinterest, you let photos do the talking for your products and services, and get customers in less than a minute.

Like Facebook, Pinterest also allows users to follow your company or comment on your page. You can use this as an advantage to connect with potential customers, build stronger relationships with your regular clients, drive more targeted traffic, collect valuable information from customers, know their shopping preferences, and respond to certain queries quickly. You can also place the link of your website along with your pinned photos to lead people to your official site. With limited characters for product description, Pinterest allows clients to focus more on your product images and has become a real visual hub.

Pinterest is especially perfect for companies targeting females. Studies have shown that many online female shoppers do not spend too much time reading product reviews and are more interested on surfing through a variety of fun and charming product images. If you're particularly looking to target females, you can take advantage of Pinterest to market your decorating ideas, wedding ideas, fashion and accessories, and recipes through attention-grabbing and mouth-watering pictures. Handy crafts, make-ups, perfumes, and custom clothing are also a perfect match for Pinterest. Not wanting to stereotype, pictures of cars, the latest DIY tools and beer could also be equally at home on Pinterest!

Pinterest is designed and aimed at connecting professionals. Thus, having an account on Pinterest will help you connect with other business professionals, public figures, and other influencers who may potentially help publicise your business. To raise awareness about your company, you can start following big names and popular figures. If they follow you back, you automatically gain a big plus point to your marketing strategy.

Pinterest can be the best place to expose your brand to a larger audience, attract new followers, and engage with your loyal customers at a whole new level. Unlike other social networking sites, Pinterest provides the safest venue to market your product. Since most members are professionals, you can expect more refined comments that will help build your product's image as a whole.

Trying out Twitter

Twitter is the second largest social networking site, and

has become an integral part of many people's daily activities. Internet-savvy folks usually use it to announce what they are up to and update people of their whereabouts. Some people also use it to share thoughts and inspirational quotes, promote their photo journals, and gather traffic for their blogs. Business professionals and entrepreneurs have also taken advantage of Twitter's versatility to connect with potential customers, increase engagement with their devoted clients, and boost up their branding strategy.

Twitter helps entrepreneurs enhance their online business in a myriad of interesting ways. It can be the best venue to create a richer experience for your audience through: visual branding, prominent featuring of the most recent updates, and encouraging more traffic to visit business campaigns, news, and other offers. With exceptional functionality and countless potential followers, it could be the key to your business's online marketing strategy.

You can start by creating a business profile to customise your brand and create awareness about your products and services. Since your profile is automatically set as public, other users can view it without joining or logging into Twitter. Every day, your profile page can be seen by thousands of potential buyers - half of them may become your avid fans.

There are three ways you can enhance your Twitter profile to increase your followers and promote your company. First, you can communicate with more users by sharing significant updates. You can use 'Hash Tags' to highlight your products and '@username' to guide customers to engage influencers and lead clients to a more exciting brand experience on your profile page. Secondly, you can take advantage of its limited characters for every Tweet to offer exclusive content in small amounts, such as product launches, breaking news, new offers and promotions, and real-time messages. Thirdly, you can

Tweet a link, video, or photo of your own products or services from a partner provider. The more interesting your Tweets are, the more chance there is that your content could be re-Tweeted by your followers. Re-Tweeting is a significant feature of Twitter that will relay your product or message to a wider audience beyond your initial fan base, which is excellent for expansion and growth.

Even with an existing Facebook account, you can have Twitter as your second supporting strategy to promote your brand. With a marketing strategy that is easy to adapt from Facebook, Twitter can be the key to drive your business endeavours forward at a whole new rate. Like Facebook, you can use Twitter to help clients solve their problems, answer relevant questions, share practical tips, and give quality advice. By using short yet catchy phrases, you can also lead a specific crowd of people from Twitter to your Facebook account and create a back-to-back marketing strategy that will make clients stick to your business. Complete with blogging and micro-blogging tools, Twitter can also help build your brand's identity. Another thing that you can do with the site is connect with top supporters and prominent influencers who may potentially increase your business appeal, and increase your engagement across different cultures and continents.

When you're using Twitter, you have to remember an important element known as 'efficiency.' It is important that you share the core values that set your company apart from others; create a business page that reflects your corporate visual identity, and Tweet on a daily basis so as to give your clients an idea of what is happening. Achieving a good Twitter strategy coupled with this element can make your Twitter account an outstanding social networking site to sustain brand loyalty from target customers. Combine it with Facebook, and we're on to a winner!

Other Resources

There are millions of websites on the Internet, many of them claiming to have the best advice for those looking for Facebook business tips and tricks. We all know however, that these websites are not all as legitimate as others. The following list offers itself as an initial guide for further research and advice, but please do bear in mind what I mentioned in my TED talk. If you find a resource that is talking about your customers as if they were a piece of meat, please close the browser window and send me an email instead. I'd rather help each and every one of you individually, than to let you go implementing terrible advice from somebody who couldn't care less about you, or your customers. Anyway, here's my list of places that are (fairly) reliable. If you spot any bad advice, let me know, and the list will be shortened in the next edition!

Lewis Love – lewislove.co.uk

Likeable Media - likeable.com
SEOMoz – seomoz.org
Social Media Examiner – socialmediaexaminer.com
Site Visibility - sitevisibility.co.uk

This list is by no means exhaustive and you may find that I've missed out your favourite book or blog. If this is the case, I do not apologise. This is my book, not yours!

Thank you for reading my book. I hope you've enjoyed it as much as I enjoyed writing it. I intend to write more books on the subject of social media and business. I'd love to let you know as and when these become available and be able to offer you an exclusive discount. Just get in contact with me to let me know your thoughts on this book, and I'll add you to my list of favourite people to contact upon future releases.

Thanks again for reading, and good luck!

ABOUT THE AUTHOR

Lewis Love is a new media consultant based in Derbyshire, UK. Originally from Essex, Lewis worked on the breakfast show of a radio station for 18 months before travelling around the world. Upon his return, he moved to the midlands to study Media Studies at the University of Derby. He was the student representative for his course for three years, and in 2012, he was awarded the University of Derby Award Student of the Year for his work with local businesses. Since then, he's worked with start-ups in the fashion industry to multi-national corporations, advising, educating and occasionally amusing them on how best to implement digital marketing strategies and enhance their online presence.

Besides his work online, Lewis enjoys spending time with his girlfriend, Emily, whom he lives with in Derby. He's an Arsenal fan, although he kindly asks you not to hold that against him, and he enjoys a craft beer from time to time; produced by smaller, passionate breweries of course.

3100704R00041

Printed in Great Britain
by Amazon.co.uk, Ltd.,
Marston Gate.